AF270686

Italy

by Julie Murray

abdobooks.com

Published by Abdo Kids, a division of ABDO, P.O. Box 398166, Minneapolis, Minnesota 55439.
Copyright © 2023 by Abdo Consulting Group, Inc. International copyrights reserved in all countries.
No part of this book may be reproduced in any form without written permission from the publisher.
Abdo Kids Jumbo™ is a trademark and logo of Abdo Kids.

Printed in the United States of America, North Mankato, Minnesota.

052022

092022

Photo Credits: Getty Images, Shutterstock

Production Contributors: Teddy Borth, Jennie Forsberg, Grace Hansen
Design Contributors: Candice Keimig, Pakou Moua

Library of Congress Control Number: 2021950551
Publisher's Cataloging-in-Publication Data

Names: Murray, Julie, author.

Title: Italy / by Julie Murray.

Description: Minneapolis, Minnesota : Abdo Kids, 2023 | Series: Countries | Includes online resources and
    index.

Identifiers: ISBN 9781098261696 (lib. bdg.) | ISBN 9781098262532 (ebook) | ISBN 9781098262952
    (Read-to-Me ebook)

Subjects: LCSH: Italy--Juvenile literature. | Italy--History--Juvenile literature. | Europe--Juvenile literature.
    | Geography--Juvenile literature.

Classification: DDC 945--dc23

Table of Contents

Italy

Italy is in Europe. It is home to more than 60 million people. Rome is Italy's capital and largest city. It is rich in history and has many famous buildings.

Geography

Four countries border Italy to the north. The rest of the country is surrounded by the Mediterranean Sea. It is a boot-shaped **peninsula**.

Europe
Africa
France
Switzerland
Austria
Slovenia
Italy
Rome
Mediterranean Sea
7

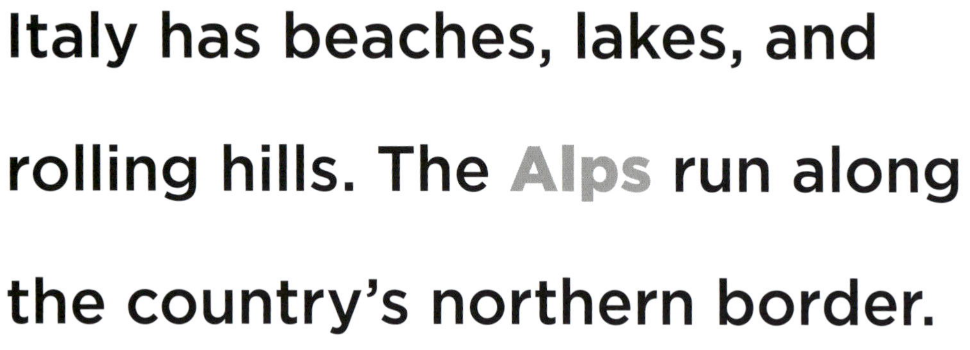

Italy has beaches, lakes, and rolling hills. The **Alps** run along the country's northern border.

Italy has about 450 islands. Mount Etna is on the island of Sicily. It is one of the most active volcanoes in the world.

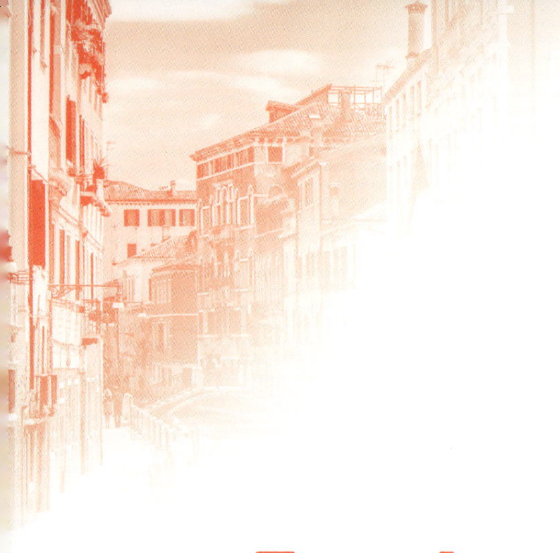

Food

Italy is known for its delicious and fresh pastas and pizza. Gelato is a popular frozen dessert.

Famous Sites

The Colosseum is in Rome. It was built in 80 CE. It is an **amphitheater** that held 50,000 people. **Gladiator** fights took place there.

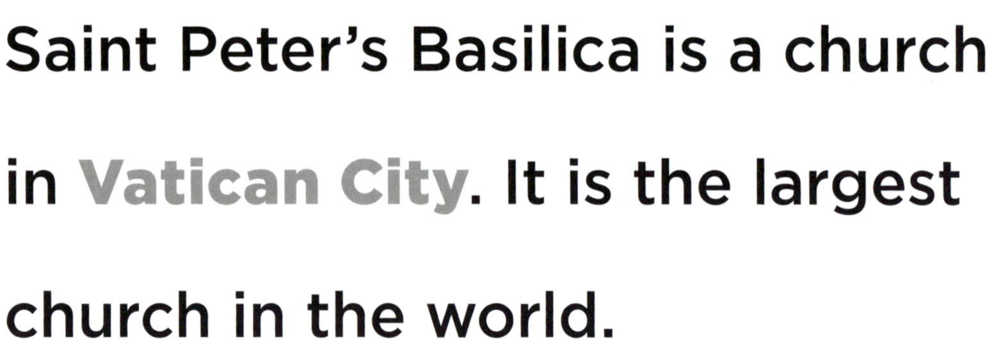

Saint Peter's Basilica is a church in **Vatican City**. It is the largest church in the world.

REM PRINCIPIS APOST PAVLVS V BVRGHESIVS ROMANVS PONT MAX AN MD CXII PONT VII
ALEXAN VII P M
L'ingresso in Basilica terminerà
alle ore 12.30

The entrance to the Basilica
will end at 12.30 pm

Famous People

Two of the most famous artists
to ever live were from Italy.
Michelangelo was a painter and
a sculptor. He is best known for
painting the Sistine Chapel.

18

Michelangelo

Leonardo da Vinci's paintings were dramatic. The *Mona Lisa* and *The Last Supper* are his most famous works.

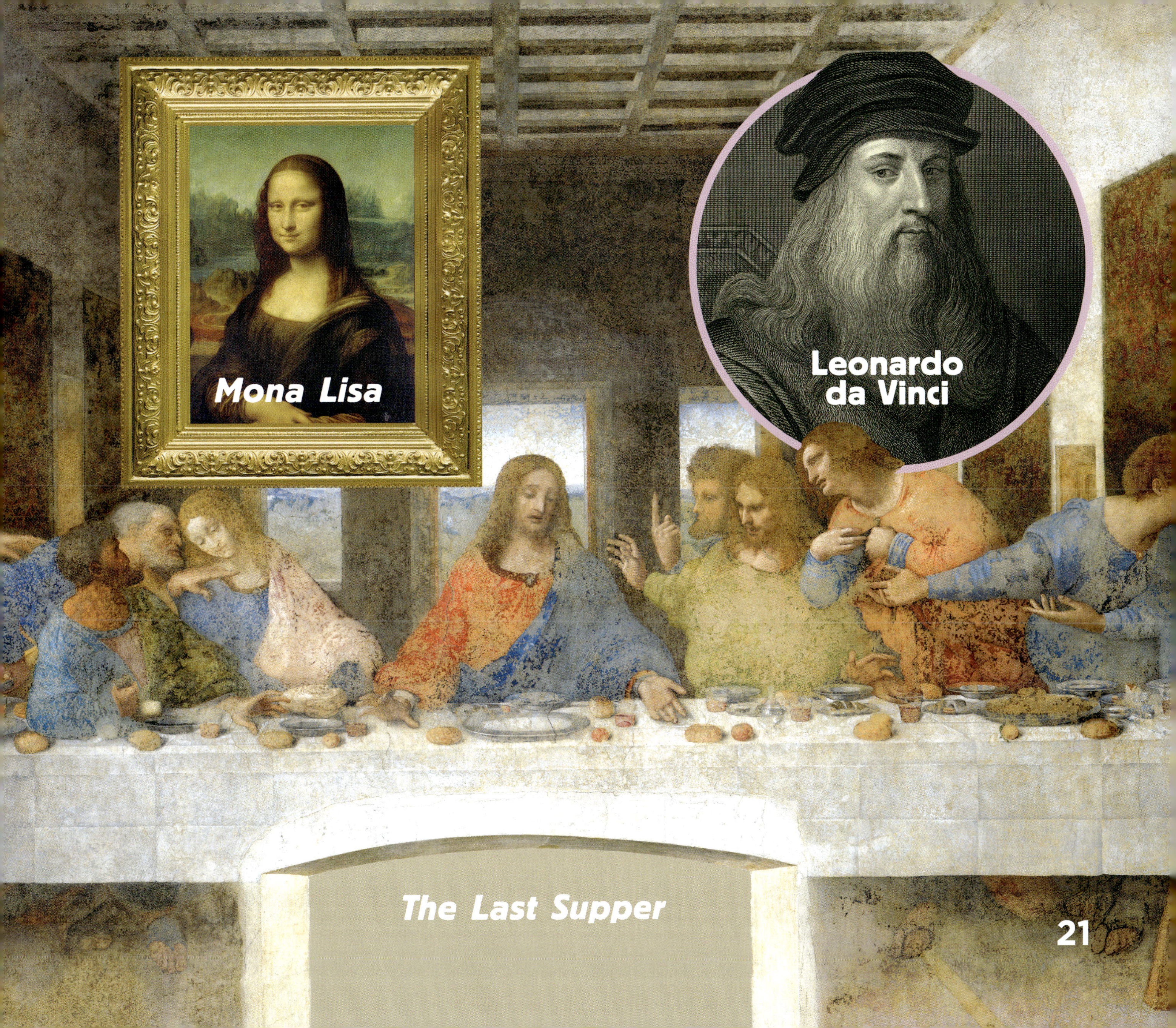

Mona Lisa
Leonardo da Vinci
The Last Supper

Awesome Landmarks

Grand Canal
Venice, Italy

Pompeii Ruins
Campania, Italy

Roman Forum
Rome, Italy

Trevi Fountain
Rome, Italy

Glossary

Alps – a high mountain range that goes from southern France through Switzerland, Italy, Germany, and Austria and into Albania.

amphitheater – an oval or round building with seats rising in rows from an open, central area.

gladiator – a man in ancient Rome who fought other men, often to the death, to entertain an audience.

peninsula – a piece of land surrounded on nearly all sides by water. It is connected to a larger body of land.

Vatican City – an independent city-state located within Rome, Italy. It has a population of about 825. It is ruled by the pope who is the bishop of Rome and the head of the Catholic Church.

Index

Abdo Kids ONLINE
FREE! ONLINE MULTIMEDIA RESOURCES

Visit **abdokids.com** to access crafts, games, videos, and more!